Words of the Master

(SELECTED PRECEPTS OF RAMAKRISHNA)

COMPILED BY

SWAMI BRAHMANANDA

ELEVENTH EDITION

1951

UDBODHAN OFFICE, BAGHBAZAR,
CALCUTTA

Price 12 As.   Cloth-Bound Re. 1/8/-

Published by
Swami Atmabodhananda
UDBODHAN OFFICE
1, Udbodhan Lane, Baghbazar
Calcutta.

Printed by
Debendra Nath Seal,
SREEKRISHNA PRINTING WORKS,
27B, Grey Street, Calcutta.

INTRODUCTION

The present brochure is from the pen of one who was regarded by the Master as next to the Swami Vivekananda in his capacity for realising religious ideals. And everyone who had the great fortune to come directly under the hallowed touch of the Mahâpurusha of Dakshineswara, can sestify to the great love which Sri Ramakrishna always bore towards the author of the volume. Indeed, if the Swami Vivekananda was loved and cherished by the Master as the instrument by which to proclaim to the world his great Mission in the realm of religion—the Swami Brahmananda was no less regarded by him as the person to fill in an important and very responsible place in the scheme of his religious organisation.

The little volume, therefore, assumes a great importance in consideration of the source from which it has come. For the only motive which has moved the author to com-pile these selected sayings of the Master is to present them to the public, as nearly as possible, in the form in which they were originally uttered. It is indeed the labour of grateful love of the beloved disciple, than whom no one used to live so constantly with the Master, to set him at his rights before the public, seeing how his invaluable words are becoming roughly handled, deformed and distorted now-a-days, at the hands of many. Well may be expected, therefore, that the attempt will be hailed by the public with delight and appreciated according to its proper merits. We need hardly point out here that the original brochure is in Vernacular (Bengali), of which we present the reader herein an English rendering. And we take this opportunity to express our sincere thanks to Srijut Jnanendra Nath Mukherji, M. A. and Mr. F. J. Alexandar for enabling us to do the same.

SARADANANDA

CONTENTS

CONTENTS

WORDS OF THE MASTER

(SELECTED PRECEPTS OF SRI RAMAKRISHNA)

KNOWLEDGE OF SELF

1. Know yourself and you shall then know God. What is my ego ? Is it my hand or foot or flesh or blood or any other part of my body ? Reflect well and you will know that there is no such thing as 'I'. The more you peel off the skin of an onion, the more skin only appears—you cannot get any kernel ; so when you analyse the ego, it vanishes away into nothingness. What is ultimately left behind is the *Atman* (soul)— the pure *Chit* (Knowledge-Absolute). God appears when the ego dies.

2. There are two egoes—one ripe (*pukkâ*) and the other unripe (*kânchâ*). "This is my house, my room, my son"—the ego that

has this idea is unripe ; while the ripe-ego is
that which thinks—"I am the servant of the
Lord, I am His child, I am ever free and
all-knowing."

3. A certain person asked Sri Ramakrishna, "Kindly instruct me in one word so
that I may be illumined." To which he
replied, "The Absolute is the only reality ;
the universe is unreal"—realise this and then
sit silent.

4. A person's egoism never leaves him
altogether so long as he possesses a body ;
some trace is always left behind. The leaves
of the cocoa-palm fall off, but leave their
marks behind on the trunk. So also with
one's egoism. But this slight egoism does
not fetter one who is already free.

5. Sri Ramakrishna put to Nyângta (the
naked) Tota Puri the question : "Where is the
necessity of daily meditation in your present
advanced state ?" Tota replied that a brass-
vessel would lose its lustre unless scrubbed
every day ; one's mind could not be kept
pure without daily meditation. Sri Rama-

krishna rejoined that if the vessel was made
of gold it would not be tarnished. That is
to say, devotional exercises were no longer
necessary for one who had come to know
God.

6. There are two kinds of reasoning—
Involution and Evolution. Of the shell of
a fruit is the kernel; so of the kernel is
the shell.

7. The idea of the ego involves that of
the non-ego. He who has an idea of light
has also an idea of darkness. He who has
a sense of sin has also a sense of virtue. He
who has a sense of right has also a sense
of wrong.

8. You can safely walk upon thorns with
your shoes on ; shod with spiritual knowledge
you can as safely roam over this thorny world.

9. There was a holy man who used to
live in a state of ecstasy and would not speak
with any one. He was regarded as a lunatic.
One day having begged some food in the
village, he took his seat by the side of a dog
and fell to eating. A strange sight now

presented itself and attracted a crowd of
spectators, for the holy man would put one
morsel into his own mouth and the next into
that of the dog, so that the man and the beast
went on eating together like a pair of friends.
Some of the spectators began to laugh at the
holy man as being a mad fellow. Thereupon
he said, "Why do you laugh ?

> Vishnu is seated with Vishnu,
> Vishnu is feeding Vishnu ;
> Why do you laugh, O Vishnu ?
> Whatever is, is Vishnu."

10. It is ignorance that leads one to seek
for God outside oneself. When one feels
that God is within oneself, it is knowledge.
He who has it here (i.e., feels the presence
of God within himself), has it also there (i.e.,
has his place at His lotus-feet).

GOD

1. Do you know how God dwells in man? He dwells in the same way as ladies of wealthy families do behind a latticed screen (*chick*). They can see everybody, but no one can see them. God abides in all in an exactly similar way.

2. It is the nature of the lamp to give light. With its help some may cook food, some may forge deeds and some may read the *Bhâgavata* (*Holy Scriptures*). Is it the fault of the light? So is it the fault of God that some try to attain salvation with the help of His holy name, while others use His name for success in attempted theft?

3. You get what you seek. God is like the *Kalpataru* (the celestial tree)—everyone gets from Him what he seeks. A poor man's son having received education and become a judge of the High Court is apt to think that he is all right. God also echoes

his thought and says, "Do thou continue so."
Afterwards when the same judge has retired
on a pension, he begins to see things in their
true light and puts to himself the question :
"What real work have I done in this life ?"
God, too, echoes his words and says : "Yes,
very true ; what hast thou done ?"

4. There is no distinction between
Impersonal God (*Brahman*) on the one hand
and Personal God (*Shakti*) on the other.
When the Supreme Being is thought of as
inactive, He is styled God the Absolute
(*Suddha Brahman*) ; and when He is
thought of as active—creating, sustaining and
destroying—He is styled *Shakti* or the
Personal God.

5. One day in course of a conversation
about God, Mathoor Babu* observed, "God,
too, is bound by the laws of nature ; He
cannot act just as He wishes." Sri Ramakrishna said, "How can that be so ? He
acts just as He pleases, He can do anything

*Son-in-law of Rani Rashmani, the foundress of the
Dakshineswar Temple.

He likes." Mathoor Babu said, "Can He
produce white flowers on this red hibiscus
plant by His mere wish ?" Sri Ramakrishna
replied, "Certainly He can do that. If it be
His wish, this red hibiscus plant shall bear
white flowers." But Mathoor did not seem
to be fully convinced. As a matter of fact,
however, in a few days, it was seen that an
hibiscus plant in the Dakshineswar Garden
bore two flowers—one red and the other
white—on two different branches. Sri Ramakrishna carried the main branch, along with
the two offshoots bearing the flowers, to
Mathoor, who felt highly suprised and ex-
claimed, "Father, I will never more argue a
point with Thee."

6. Have you any idea of God with form
and God without form ? They are like ice
and water. When water freezes into ice, it
has a form ; when the same ice is melted
into water, all form is lost.

7. Tears were flowing out of the eyes
of Bishmadeva when he was lying stretched
on his bed of arrows waiting for death.

On seeing this *Arjuna* remarked to the Lord *Sri Krishna*, "Brother, how strange! My grandfather who is ever truthful, whose passions are under control, who is full of Divine knowledge and is himself one of the eight *Vasus*, (a class of minor Deities)—he, too, is found shedding tears under the influence of *Mâyâ* (delusion)!" On the Lord's mentioning this to *Bhishmadeva*, the latter said, "O Krishna, Thou knowest full well that I am not weeping through *Mâyâ*. The thought that I cannot in the least comprehend the nature of Thy *leelâ* (sport), is what makes me weep. The Lord, by repeating Whose holy names men surmount all dangers, has Himself been acting as the charioteer of the *Pândavas* and befriending them and yet there is no end to their trials."

8. Sri Ramakrishna accompained Mathoor Babu on his pilgrimage to Benares. While stopping at that city, Sri Ramakrishna paid a visit to Trailanga Swami, to whom he put the question, "How is it that people speak of so many Gods although there is but one

God ?" The Swami was observing a vow of
silence ; so he merely raised one of his fingers
and threw himself into a sort of trance,
hinting thereby that by meditation one comes
to know that there is only one God, but by
philosophical discussion the sense of unity is
displaced by a sense of diversity.

9. God with form and God without
form are not two different Beings. He Who
is with form is also without form. To a
devotee God manifests Himself in various
forms. Just think of a shoreless ocean—an
infinite expanse of water—no land visible
in any direction ; only here and there are
visible blocks of ice formed by intense cold.
Similarly, under the cooling influence, so to
say, of the deep devotion of his worshipper,
the Infinite reduces Himself into the Finite
and appears before him as a Being with
form. Again, as on the appearance of the
sun, the ice melts away, so on the appearance
of the sun of knowledge, God with form
melts away into the formless.

SELF-DELUSION (MAYA)

1. Well, what do you think of the nature of Mâyâ? It is like the weeds floating on a pond. You can push away the weeds, but presently the cleared space will fill in again. Similarly, so long as you reason within yourself and associate with holy men, everything seem clear; but shortly afterwards worldly desires will throw over you the veil of illusion.

2. The snake has poison in its fangs, but it is none the worse for it. The poison does not affect it or cause its death. It is poison in relation to other creatures whom it may chance to bite. Similarly, although the phenomenal universe exists in God, He is above and beyond it. The universe of phenomena exists as such only for us.

3. What is the difference between Mâyâ (self-love) and Dayâ (charity)? Mâyâ is attachment and love towards one's own relations

and friends—parents, brother, sister, wife,
children, nephew, niece, etc. *Dayâ* is love
extending equally to all beings ; it proceeds
from the knowledge that God abides in all.

4. If the person possessed by an evil spirit
has the consciousness that he is so possessed,
the evil spirit at once leaves him. Similarly,
the *Jiva* (individual soul) possessed by the
spirit of Mâyâ (self-delusion), on realising that
he is self-deluded, becomes at once free from
Mâyâ.

5. It is the veil of Mâyâ that keeps God
hidden from our sight. The Universal Soul
(*Paramâtmâ*) cannot be realized till this veil
is removed. As for instance, suppose *Râma*
is only a few steps ahead of *Lakshmana*, and
Seetâ is between the two. Here *Râma* stands
for the Universal Soul, *Lakshmana* for the
individual soul (*Jiva*) and *Seetâ* is the Mâyâ.
So long as the Mother *Jânaki* (*Seetâ*) is between the other two, *Lakshmana* cannot see
Râma. It is only when She stands aside a
little that *Lakshmana* can see *Râma*.

6. *Mâyâ* is of two kinds—one leading

towards God (*Vidyâ-Mâyâ*) and the other leading away from God (*Avidyâ-Mâyâ*). *Vidyâ-Mâyâ* again is of two kinds—discrimination and non-attachment. With the help of these, individual souls (*Jiva*) surrender themselves to the mercy of God. *Avidyâ-Mâyâ* is of six kinds—lust, anger, avarice, inordinate attachment, pride and envy. This kind of *Mâyâ* gives rise to the sense of 'I and mine' and serves to keep men chained to the world. But as soon as *Vidyâ-Mâyâ* manifests itself, all *Avidyâ-Mâyâ* is totally destroyed.

7. The sun or the moon cannot be properly reflected in turbid water, like-wise the Universal Soul cannot be properly realised so long as the veil of *Mâyâ* is not removed *i. e.*, so long as the sense of 'I and mine' is not gone.

8. The sun lights up the earth, but a small cloud will hide it from our view. Similarly the insignificant veil of *Mâyâ* prevents us from seeing the Omnipresent and All-witnessing *Sachchidânanda* (Existence-Knowledge-Bliss).

9. If you push away the weeds on pond,
the floating matter will presently return to its
old position. In the same manner, if you
push away Mâyâ, it will return to you in a
short time. But then, just as you could prevent
the return of the weeds by interposing a piece
of floating bamboo in their way, so also could
you prevent the return of Mâyâ by the fence
of knowledge and love of God. In that case
Mâyâ could not make its way through such
obstacle—Sachchidânanda (Existence-Knowledge-Bliss) alone would be perceived.

10. A certain Sâdhu (holy man) lived
for some time in the room above the nahabat-
khânâ (concert-room) of the Temple of
Dakshineswar. He did not speak with
anybody and spent his whole time in meditation of God. One day, all of a sudden,
a cloud darkened the sky and shortly afterwards a high wind blew away the cloud.
The holy man now came out of his room and
began to laugh and dance in the verandah in
front of the concert-room. Upon this Sri
Ramkarishna asked him : "How is it that you

who spend your days so quietly in your room,
are dancing in joy and feel so jolly to day ?"
The holy man replied, "Such is the *Mâyâ*
that envelopes this life !" At first there is
the clear sky, all of a sudden a cloud darkens
it and presently everything is as before once
more.

INCARNATIONS OF GOD

(AVATARA)

1. A mighty raft of wood floating down a river carries on it hundreds and does not sink. A small piece of wood floating down may sink with the weight of a crow. So when a Saviour incarnates, hundreds find salvation through His grace. The *Siddha* (perfect man) only saves himself with much toil and trouble.

2. The locomotive engin reaches the destination itself and also draws and takes with it a long train of loaded wagons. Incarnations of God in like manner carry multitudes of men to the foot-stool of God.

DIFFERENT STAGES OF MAN

1. Man is like a pillow-case. The colour of one pillow-case may be red, that of another black and so on, but all contain the same cotton. So it is with man—one is handsome, another is ugly, a third pious, a fourth wicked but the Divine One dwells within them all.

2. One meets with two classes of men ; the nature of one resembles that of the winnowing fan and of the other that of the sieve. Just as the winnowing basket rejects the useless (husk) and keeps the useful (grain), so there is one class of men who reject what is worthless (gold, lust, &c.) and accepts the Lord, Who alone is worth having. Again as the sieve rejects the finer parts of a substance and keeps the coarser, so there is another class of men who reject what alone is worth having, and instead accept gold, lust, &c.

3. The mind of the worldly is like the bettle. The bettle loves to live in cowdung ;

it does not like to live in any other element. It will feel very uneasy if you force it into a fragrant lotus. Similarly, the worldly-minded do not care for anything else except a talk about wordly things. They will leave the place where people are found talking about God and matters spiritual and find peace by betaking themselves to a place where idle gossip is going on.

4. As when fishes are caught in a net, some do not struggle at all but remain calm in the net, some again struggle hard to come out of the net but fail in the attempt, while a third set actually effect their escape by rending the net ; so there are three classes of men in this world—the bound (*baddha*), the struggling (*mumukshu*) and the released (*mukta*).

5. A fisherwoman on her way home was overtaken by a storm at nightfall ; so she took refuge in a florist's house. The florist received her very kindly and allowed her to pass the night on the porch adjoining the room in which he kept his flowers. But, although thus comfortably lodged, she could not get a

2

wink of sleep. At last she discovered that the
sweet aroma of the flowers in the garden was
what had kept her awake. She, therofore,
sprinkled some water on her empty basket of
fish and placed it close to her nose. In a
short time she fell into a sound sleep. Similar is the case with the worldly-minded. They,
too, relish nothing else except the foul smell
of the putrid things of the world.

6. By talking with a worldly man one can
feel that his heart is filled with worldly
thoughts and desires, just as one can feel that
the crop of a young pigeon is full of grains.
Worldliness is what men of this order care
about ; they do not like to hear religious
discourses.

7. If a person has eaten radishes, the
smell of his eructations will betray the fact.
Similarly, if you meet with a pious man he
will presently begin to talk on spiritual sub-
ject ; on the other hand, worldly man will
talk only about worldly things.

8. There are two kinds of flies. One is
the honoy-bee that sucks honey only ; the

other not only sucks honey, but will preferab-
ly sit on an unclean sore when it gets the
opportunity. So with men. Those who love
God cannot talk on any other theme but God,
while those that are attached to things of
the world, at once jump into a conversation
about lust and gold, should such be started,
discarding the words about God which they
had been listening to.

9. The characteristic of a thoroughly
worldly man is that he does not only not
listen to hymns, religious discourses, praises
of the Almighty &c, but also prevents others
from hearing them and abuses religion and
religious men, and scoffs at those who mediate
upon God.

10. The alligator has such a thick skin
that no weapon can pierce it. So, how-much-
so-ever you may preach religion to a worldly
man, it will have no effect upon his heart.

11. The sun's light falls equally on all
surfaces, but only bright surfaces like water,
mirrors and polished metals, can reflect it fully. In like manner, although God abides in

all, He manifests Himself most in the hearts
of the pious.

12.   A number of cakes may have the same
look, but may be stuffed with different in-
gredients, e.g., some may contain the kernel
of the cocoanut, some others sweet condensed
milk (*ksheera*), and so on.   Similarly, though
all human bodies are made of the same
materials, yet men differ from one another
owing to a difference in their qualities.

13.   All   water is *Nârâyana* (God), but
every kind of water is not fit to drink.   Similarly, though it is true that the Almighty
dwells in evey place, yet every place is not fit
to be visited.   As one kind of water may be
used for washing your feet, another for rinsing
your mouth, a third may be drunk, while a
certain other again may not even be touched ;
similarly, some places are fit to be visited,
some only to be saluted from a distance and
bidden good-bye, and so on.

14.   True it is that God dwells even in the
tiger, but we must not go and face the animal.
So it is true that God dwells even in the most

wicked, but it is not meet that we should associate with them.

15. A certain *guru* (spiritual guide) taught his disciple that every created thing was *Nârâyana* (God), and the disciple took him at his word. One day the disciple met an elephant on the street. The animal was advancing towards him and the driver (*mâhut*) was shouting, "Move away! move away!" The disciple argued in his mind, "Why should I move away? I am *Nârâyana*, so is the elephant; what fear has *Nârâyana* for Himself?" Thinking thus, he did not move. At last the elephant took him up in his trunk and dashed him aside. He was hurt severely, and going back to his master he related the whole adventure. The *guru* said, "Well said, my son! You are *Nârâyana* and so is the elephant; but why did you not pay heed to the warnings of the *mâhut-Nârâyana* (driver-God) who had asked you to move away?"

16. The anger of the good is like a line which is drawn on the surface of water and which soon disappears.

17. A *Brâhmana's* son is no doubt a *Brâhmana* by birth ; but some born of *Brâhmanas* grow up into learned scholars, become priests, others turn out cooks, and some others, yet again, roll themselves in dust in front of a courtesan's door.

18. Gold is distinguished from brass by the touchstone ; similarly, human nature—whether one is sincere or insincere—is tested by God.

19. Men are of two classes—men in name only (*mânush*) and knowing-men (*mân-hunsh*). Those alone who thirst after God belong to the latter class ; those that are mad after lust and gold are all ordinary men.

20. Nothing will rouse up the worldly-minded. They suffer from no end of pain and trouble in this life, still they do not get any the wiser. Just think of the camel. It is fond of thorns and will not forbear from eating them, blood trickling down its mouth notwithstanding. Similarly, the worldly-minded do not take to heart even a great bereavement, and in a few days feel and act as if nothing had happened.

21. Beware of the followings—(1) of him whose words flow like water ; (2) of him the door of whose heart is sealed ; (3) of the devotee who shows off to the world his devotion by the sacred *tulasi*-leaf stuck on the ear ; (4) of the woman who wears a long veil ; (5) of the tank covered with weeds, the cold water of which is so injurious to health.

GURU (SPIRITUAL GUIDE)

1. The *Guru* is only one, but *Upa-Gurus* (secondary *gurus*) may be many. He is an *Upa-Guru* from whom anything whatsoever is learned. It is mentioned in the *Bhagavata* that the great *Avadhuta* (a great *yogi*) had twenty-four such *Upa-Gurus*.

2. One day as the *Avadhuta* was walking across a meadow, he saw a bridal procession coming towards him with loud beating of drums and great pomp. Hard by he saw a hunter deeply absorbed in aiming at his game and perfectly inattentive to the noise and pomp of the procession, casting not even a passing look at it. The *Avadhuta*, saluting the hunter, said, "Sir, thou art my *Guru*. When I sit in meditation, let my mind be concentrated upon the object of meditation as thine has been on your game."

3. An angler was fishing in a pond. The *Avadhuta* approaching him asked, "Brother,

which way leads to such and such a place ?"
The float of the rod at that time was indicating
that the fish was nibling at the bait ; so the
man did not give any reply but was all attention to his fishing rod. Having first hooked
the fish, he turned round and said, "What
is it you have been saying, sir ?" The *Avadhuta*
saluted him and said, "Sir, thou art my *Guru*.
When I sit in the contemplation of the Deity
of my choice (*Ishta*), let me follow thy example
and before finishing my devotions let me not
attened to anything else."

4. A kite with a fish in its beak was
followed by a host of crows and other
kites, which were pecking at it and trying to
snatch the fish away. In whatever direction
it went, its tormentors followed it cawing,
till at last they made it let go the fish in
vexation. Another kite instantly caught the
fish and was in its turn followed by the whole
lot. The first kite was left unmolested and
sat calmly on the branch of a tree. Seeing
this quiet and tranquil state of the bird the
Avadhuta saluting him, said, "Thou art my

Guru, for thou hast taught me that peace of mind is possible in this world, only when one has given up one's adjuncts (*upâdhi*); otherwise there is danger at every step."

5. A heron was slowly walking on a marsh to catch a fish. Behind, there was a fowler aiming an arrow at the heron, but the bird was totally unmindful of this fact. The *Avadhuta* saluting the heron, said, "When I sit in meditation, let me follow thy examaple and never turn back to see who is behind me."

6. The *Avadhuta* found another *Guru* in a bee. The bee had been storing up honey with long and great labour. A man came from somewhere, broke the hive and drank up the honey. The bee was not destined to enjoy the fruit of its long labour. On seeing this, the *Avadhuta* saluted the bee, saying, "Lord ! Thou art my *Guru*; from Thee I learn what is the sure fate of accumulated riches."

7. "Men as spiritual guides can be had by

hundreds of thousands, but it is hard to get a single disciple,"—is an ancient saying. Many are the persons who can give good advice, but few there are who care to follow it.

8. Should a genuine love of God come to a person and should he be anxious to perform devotional exercises, God would surely provide him with a properly qualified *Guru*. There need be no anxiety about one.

9. Doctors are either first class, second class or third class. The third class doctor feels the pulse of the patient and advises him to take some drug ; he then goes away and does not care to enquire if the patient actually takes the medicine or not. The second class doctor tries to impress on his patient that he will come round by using the medicine prescribed and adopts all gentle means to induce his unwilling patient to take it. The first class doctor, when he finds that his patient is determined not to take any medicine, does not hesitate to put his knee on the chest of the patient and force the medicine down his gullet. In like manner, the *Guru* who,

having given religious instruction to his disciple, takes no further notice of him, is a Guru of the third class. He who, for the sake of the disciple's good, hammers his instructions into him till they are grasped and shows that he is interested in the disciple's welfare, is a Guru of the second class. And he who, finding that his disciple does not properly listen to or follow his teachings, enforces obedience by compulsion, is a Guru of the first class.

RELIGION IS REALISATION AND NOT A MATTER FOR PHILOSOPHICAL DISCUSSION

1. How long does one need to discuss the contents of the scriptures ? Only until one has succeeded in seeing the Lord. The bee will buzz so long as it does not settle upon the flower. As soon as it begins to drink of the honey, all buzzing is at an end.

2. One day the late Keshab Chandra sen of revered memory visited Sri Ramakrishna in the temple of Dakshineswara and put to him the question : "Many learned men read no end of sacred books ; how is it then, that they remain ignorant in spiritual matters ?" The reply was, "The kite and the vulture soar high up in the air, but all the time their eyes are fixed on charnel pits in search of putrid carcasses. The minds of the so-called learned scholars are attached to things of the world ; hence it is that they cannot

acquire true knowledge. What good could the reading of a vast number of sacred works do them ?"

3. Sri Ramakrishna used to say of *granthas* (books) that they were so many *granthis* (knots). In other words, mere reading of books, without discrimination and non-attachment, serves to increase one's arrogance and vanity, *i. e.*, it multiplies the knots in one's mind.

4. Sri Ramakrishna once told a gentleman who was very fond of disputation, "If one word will satisfy you, then come to me ; but if you want to understand the Truth after a long disputation, then go to Keshab Chandra Sen."

5. When a pitcher is being filled, a gurgling sound (*bhak, bhak*) is heard ; as soon as it is full, the sound ceases. Similarly, the man who has not found God is full of vain disputations about Him. But he who has seen Him silently enjoys the Bliss Divine.

6. It is useless to pore over the sacred books if there is no discrimination (*Viveka*)

or non-attachment (*Vairāgya*). No spiritual progress can be made without these. *Viveka* means discrimination between the Real (God) and the unreal (phenomenal universe) and adherence to the Real. The knowledge that the soul is distinct from the physical body, is also called *Viveka*. Non-attachment to things of the world is called *Vairāgya*.

7. In the Hindu almanac it is recorded that the rainfall will reach twenty âdas (*āda* is a measure of capacity used in Bengal). Wring the almanac, so full of rain-predictions, but not a drop of water can be got out of it. So, also, many good sayings are to be found in the sacred books, but the mere reading of them will not make one spiritual. One must go through the practices enjoined in them.

8. Two men went into an orchard. As soon as the worldly-wise man entered the gate, he began to count the number of mango-trees, the number of mangoes each tree bore, etc., and calculate what might be the price of the orchard. His companion went to the owner,

made his acquaintance and quietly going under a mango tree, began to pluck the fruit and eat it with the owner's consent. Now, who is the wiser of the two ? Eat mangoes ; it will satisfy your hunger. What is the good of counting the leaves and of making useless calculations ? The proud man of intellect is busy with all sorts of vain discussion and controversies regarding God, while the humble man of wisdom having received God's grace enjoys supreme bliss in this world.

9. So long as a man is far away from the market, he hears only an indistinct buzzing noise like *ho ! ho !* But when he enters the market-place the sound becomes distinct. He sees that some one is bargaining, another purchasing, and so on. Similarly, one cannot realise the essence of religion so long as one is far away from the world of religion.

10. The *Vedas,* the *Purânas* and all other sacred books have with one sole exception become, as it were, defiled (*uchchhishta*), having been uttered by human mouths. That one exception is *Brahman* or the Absolute,

for no one as yet has been able to say what
it is like.

11. It is an impossible to explain to a
wordly man the nature of the ecstasy of
Divine Communion as it is to explain to a
little boy the nature of the relationship
between man and wife.

12. It is easy to utter, "do, re, mi, fa, sol,
la, si" by mouth, but not so easy to play them
on an instrument. So it is easy to talk religion
but it is difficult to practise religion.

13. A certain *Brahmachāri* (aspirant)
named Ramchandra one day visited Sri-
Ramakrishna at the temple of Dakshineswara.
The aspirant had allowed his hair to grow
into long matted tresses after the way of
Sannyāsins. Having taken his seat, he began
to exclaim from time to time : "*Shivoham !
Shivoham* (I am the Lord *Shiva !*)," but was
dumb otherwise. Sri Ramakrishna observed
him silently for some time and then remarked :
"What is the good of merely repeating the
word '*Shivoham*'? It is only when one, by
perfect meditation on the Lord in the temple

3

of one's heart, has lost all idea of self and
realised the Lord *Shiva* within, that one is
entitled to utter this sacred word. What good
can the mere repetition of the formula do
without the realisation ? So long as the stage
of realisation is not reached, it is better to
regard the Lord as the Master and oneself as
His humble servant." The aspirant came to
see his mistake and became wiser by this
advice and other similar teachings. Before he
left the place, he wrote down on the wall of
Sri Ramakrishna's room : "Taught by the
Swami, from this day forward Rama Chandra
Brahmachari regards the Lord as his Master
and himself as humble servant."

DEVOTINAL EXERCISES (SADHANA) SUITABLE FOR THE HOUSE-HOLDER

1. In the play of hide-and-seek, if the player has touched the grand-dame (*boori*), he cannot take any further part in the play ; he is free to go about wherever he chooses without being pursued and made a thief of. Similarly, in the world's play-ground one who has touched the lotus-feet of God is free from bondage. Wordly things cannot fetter him who has surrendered himself to the mercy of God.

2. In the village they lay fish-traps (*ghuni*) along waterways and in the fields. Seeing the water pass glittering through the network of bamboo-twigs, the small fry enter into it with great pleasure and having once entered, they cannot get out ; they are caught and presently lose their lives. Only one or two fishes profiting by the experience of others effect their escape by jumping away to a

different direction. Similarly, foolish men
enter into the world allured by its false glitter,
but later on they are entangled by the world's
Mâyâ and endure much suffering and are at
last annihilated. They alone enjoy real happiness and pleasure who taking lesson from the
experience of others, keep themselves aloof
from lust and gold and take refuge at the
lotus-feet of God.

3. The devotee Ramaprasada called this
world a structure of dreams ; but once a man
has acquired love for the Lord, this world is
for him—

"——a mansion of joy.
I pass my days eating, drinking
and rejoicing.
Janaka, the royal sage, how great
was his power !
Was there anything in which he was
found wanting ?"
Ah ! no, he was loyal to both (God and the
phenomenal world) ; he did give his mind to
God and at the same time drank his cup
of milk.

4. A certain person asked Sri Ramakrishna if it were possible for a house-holder
to be devoted to God. Sri Ramakrishna
smiled and replied : "In the villages about
my birthplace I have seen women preparing
cheera (flattend rice). With one hand a
woman would stir the *cheera* in the mortar
of a *dhenki* (a husking-machine), with the
other she would hold the child to her breast
and suckle it, and at the same time she would
bargain with a purchaser,—'You owe me so
much on previous account ; the charge to-day
is so much, &c.' Thus, though manifold are
her occupations, her mind is fixed on the one
idea that the pestle of the *dhenki* shall not fall
on her hand and crush it and disable it for
ever. Be in the world, but always remember
Him. You shall be lost if you turn away
from Him."

5. That man who, living in the midst of
the temptations of the world, can discipline his
mind by devotional exercises, is the true hero.
The true hero can look in any direction he
chooses, while carrying a heavy burden on his

head. Similarly, the prefect man, whose
mind is thoroughly disciplined, has his eyes
consantly directed towards God even when
he is weighed down by the burden of wordly
duties.

6. As the women in Upper India carry
four or five jars of water, placed one over the
other, upon their heads, talking with their
friends as they walk, about their joys and
sorrows, but all the while keeping their minds
fixed upon the jars that they might be safe, so
must a traveller in the path of virtue, under all
circumstances, should take heed that his heart
does not swerve from the true path.

7. As the *Baul* (street-minstrel) plays
upon two different instruments at one and the
same time ; so oh ye house-holders, perform
your various wordly duties with both your
hands, but never farget to repeat constantly
the name of the Lord.

8. As one unchaste woman, while engaged
in house-hold duties, constantly thinks of her
secret lover and of the hour of his expected
visit, even so oh ye house-holders, do your

round of wordly duties, but fix your heart always on the Lord.

9. Do you know how it is to live un-attached to the world ? One should live like the mud-fish (*pānkāl matsya*). The mud-fish live in the muddy water, but is not soiled by it.

10. The heavier scale of a balance goes down while the lighter one rises up. The human mind is like the beam of a balance, the scales of which are acted upon by two different sets of influences, *viz.*, (1) love of the world, its honours &c., and (2) discrimination, non-attachment and love of God. If the first set preponderates, the mind (like the beam of the balance) gravitates towards the world and goes away from God ; but if the second preponderates, the mind gravitates towards God and goes away from the world.

11. A husbandman was watering a sugar-cane field the whole day. After finishing his task he found that not a drop of water had entered the field ; all the water had flowed out through some distant rat-holes. Such is the state of that devotee who worships God,

but at the same time cherishes in his heart wordly desires (of wealth, fame, &c). Though he may pray every day of his life, he will find at last that he has made no progress whatever, —his entire devotion has run to waste through the rat-holes of these desires.

12. A boy holding on to a post turns round it with headlong speed. While spinning he has his attention constantly fixed on the post ; he knows very well that he will never fall down so long as he holds on to the post, but would fall directly should he let go his hold. So perform your wordly duties with your mind constantly fixed upon God and you shall be free from all dangers.

13. Many perform religious rites hoping that the amount of their wordly happiness will be increased thereby ; but they lose sight of God when any misfortune overtakes them or when they are at the point of death. Under ordinary circumstances a parrot would repeat the name of Radha-Krishna through the whole day, but when it is caught by a cat, it forgets that name and cries its natural cry.

14. There is no harm if a boat is in the water, but the water must not be allowed to get into the boat; otherwise, the boat will sink. Similarly, there is no harm if a devotee lives in the world as a house-houlder but he must not allow worldliness to enter into his mind.

15. What is the world like ? It is like the hog-plum—all skin and stone but with very little pulp—the eating of which produces colic.

16. If you rub your hands with oil and then break open the jack-fruit, the milky exudation of the fruit will not stick to your hand. So, if you first anoint your body with the oil of devotion, you can live in the world without being contaminated by lust or gold.

17. A snake bites one who attempts to catch it. But a person who has learned the art of snake-charming, can with immunity carry about seven snakes hanging about his neck and put them through many kinds of sports. Similarly, he who lives as a house-holder, after having acquired 'discrimination' and the spirit

of renunciation, can never be polluted by the
attractions of the world. Discrimination and
Renunciation are like the 'enchanted dust'
which is said to afford immunity to the snake-
charmer.

18. One's speech betrays one's thoughts
just as if you eat radishes, the smell of your
eructations will betray the fact. Similarly,
wordly-minded men talk mostly about wordly
affairs even when they visit a *sâdhu* (holy
man).

19. Know that the mind is at the root of
everything. It is the mind that makes one
wise or ignorant, bound or free, holy or
wicked, sinful or virtuous. He whose mind is
always fixed on God requires no other
spiritual exercise.

20. Do you know the condition of one
who has acquired supreme wisdom (*Brahma-
jnâna*)? Such a person sees the All-perva-
ding Spirit both within and without ; he lives,
as it were, in a room with glass-doors.

21. The result of reading the whole
of the *Bhagavata-Geetâ* is the same as that

of uttering the word *Geetâ* twelve times. Say
Geetâ, Geetâ a dozen times ; it comes to be
tyâgee tyâgee (one who has renounced). In
one word, the *Geetâ* teaches renuncaition ;
give up everything and surrender yourself to
the lotus-feet of God.

OF PERSONS QUALIFIED (ADHIKÀRI)
FOR SPIRITUAL EXERCISES
(SÁDHANA)

1. A whole mango, guava, &c. may be offered to God or may be used for other purposes ; but if it be once pecked by a crow, it can neither be offered to the Deity, nor given to a Brâhmana nor should it be eaten by any one. Similarly, boys and youths should be encouraged to seek God. They are like unpecked fruits, being totally untainted by wordly desires. Once such desires have entered into their minds, it is very difficult to make them tread the path to salvation.

2. Why do I love young-men so much ? Because they are masters of the whole (16 annas) of their minds, which get divided and sub-divided as they grow up. One half of the mind of a married man goes to his wife. When a child is born it takes away one-fourth (4 annas), and the remaining one-fourth

(4 *annas*) is scattered over parents, wordly honours, dress &c. Therefore, a young mind can easily know God. It is very difficult for old people to do so.

3. The parrot cannot be taught to sing if the membrane of its throat becomes hardened with age. It must be taught while it is young. Similarly, in old age it is difficult for the mind to be fixed on God. It can be easily done so in youth.

4. If a *seer* of adulterated milk contain a *chatâk* (sixteenth part of a *seer*) of water, it can be thickened into *kshira* (condensed milk) with very little labour and consumption of fuel. But should there be three *poás* (fourth part of a *seer*) of water in a *seer*, the milk cannot be easily thickened, and a large consumption of fuel will be required. A young mind, being but slightly adulterated with worldly desires, can be easily turned towards God ; this cannot be done with the minds of old people which are highly adulterated with such desires.

5. The tender bamboo can be easily bent,

but the full grown bamboo breaks when an attempt is made to bend it. It is easy to bend young hearts towards God, but the heart of the old escapes the hold when so drawn.

6. The human mind is like a package of mustard-seed. As it is very difficult to gather the seeds that escape out of a torn package and are scattered in all directions, so when the human mind runs in diverse directions and is occupied with many worldly things, it is not a very easy task to collect and concentrate it. The mind of a youth, not running in diverse directions, can be easily fixed on anything ; but the mind of an old man, being totally occupied with wordly things, it is very hard for him to draw it away from them and fix it on God.

7. Milk should be churned into butter before sun-rise ; you cannot get good butter by churning milk in day-time. Similarly they alone come to know God, who turn their mind God-wards and practise devotional exercises in their youth.

8. A wet match does not ignite, even by

repeated rubbing—it will simply break into
small pieces. But a dry match ignites at once,.
even with the slightest rubbing. A guileless,
honest and pure heart, untainted by worldly
desires, is like the dry match. The slightest ˙
mention of the name of the Lord kindles the
fire of love in such a heart ; but the mind of
the worldly man, soaked in lust and wealth, is
like the moist match.´ Though God may be˙
preached a hundred times, the fire of love can›
never be kindled in them.

DIFFERENT CLASSES OF ASPIRANTS
(SADHAKA)

1. One meets with two classes of aspirants —one of them resembles the young of a monkey and the other may be likened to a kitten. The young of a monkey first clasps its mother and then its mother carries it about from place to place. The kitten does not clasp its mother, but mews piteously wherever it is placed by her. Then the mother-cat comes to it and carries it wherever she chooses, holding it by the neck. Similarly, the aspirant who follows the path of knowledge or of self-less work depends upon his own effort to attain salvation. On the other hand, the aspirant who follows the path of love knows that the Lord is the disposer of everything; so with perfect confidence he resigns himself entirely to His mercy. The former is like the young of a monkey and the latter like the kitten.

2. As one master of the house appears in

differnt aspects to different members of his
family, being father to one, uncle to another,
brother-in-law to a third, father-in-law to a
fourth and so on ; similarly, one and the same
God is regarded in various aspects and worshipped in various ways by his devotees.
Some regard Him and commune with Him as
their Friend, some as Master, some as Child,
some as Husband and so on.

3.   You get what you seek. He who seeks
God gets Him ; he who seeks for wealth or
power gets that.

4.   A beggar would be acting very foolishly,
were he to go to the King's palace and beg
for such insignificant things as a gourd or a
pumpkin. Similarly, a devotee would be acting very foolishly were he to appear at the
thresh-hold of the King of Kings and beg for
such insignificant gifts as the eight psychic
powers (siddhis), neglecting the priceless gifts
of true knowledge and love of God.

5.   It is very difficult to understand the
real nature of a devotee, whether he follows
the path of love or that of knowledge. The

4

elephant has two sets of teeth—the external tusks which serve merely as ornamental appendage and the inner tusks which serve as grinders. Similarly, the devotee often-times hides his real nature and assumes some other.

16.   There are two classes of *Yógis* (devotees following the path of meditation)— hidden and open. The former go through religious practices in secret and keep themselves hidden from the public gaze. The latter carry about with them the external symbols of the *Yógis*, such as a bamboo twig and converse freely on spiritual subjects.

THE TRUE LOVER OF GOD

1. A stone may remain for thousands of years in water and the water will never penetrate it. But clay on coming in contact with water gets mixed up with it directly. So the heart of the faithful does not despair in the midst of thousands of trials, but the man of weak faith is easily shaken by the most trifling cause.

2. The Lord being pleased with *Prahlâda's* prayers and hymns, asked him what boon he desired. *Prahlâda* replied, "Lord, forgive those who oppressed me ; in punishing them Thou wilt be punishing Thyself, for verily Thou abidest in every being."

3. Sri Ramakrishna felt a strong desire to meet the saintly Keshab Chandra (Sen). Keshab Babu was then living with his disciples (the *Brâhmos*) at Belgharia in the garden-house of the late Joy Gopal Sen. Sri Ramakrishna drove to the garden, accompanied by Hriday

Mukherjee. Keshab Babu with his disciples was then getting himself ready for a bath in the garden-tank. Sri Ramakrishna pointed to Keshab Babu and remarked, "He is the only one here whose tail has dropped off." Upon this Keshab Babu's disciples burst into a loud laugh. Keshab Babu said to them in a tone of reproof, "Don't you laugh ; his words have some deep meaning." Sri Ramakrishna then explained himself as follows : "So long as the tadpole's tail does not drop off, it can live only in water ; when the tail drops off, it can live both in water and on land. Similarly, he whose tail of ignorance has dropped off by divine contemplation can both dive into the Sea of Divine Bliss and live in the world, just as he pleases."

OBSTACLES TO DEVOTIONAL EXERCISES
(SADHANA)

1. If there is a small hole in the bottom of a jar of water, the whole water flows out by and by ; similarly, if there be the slightest tinge of worldliness in the aspirant, all his exertions come to naught.

2. Soft clay admits of forms, but the burnt clay does not. So those whose hearts are burnt with the fire of wordly desires cannot be impressed with sriritual ideas.

3. Sugar and sand may be mixed together but the ant rejects the sand and eats the sugar. Similarly, pious men and *Pramahamsas* (great *Yògis*) reject the unreal (i.e., lust and gold) and choose the Real (i e., Sachchidà. nanda).

4. Paper rubbed over with oil cannot be written upon. So, the soul spoiled by the oil of sense enjoyments (lust and gold) is unfit for devotional exercises. But as oiled paper

rubbed over with chalk can be written upon, so if the soul be chalked over with renunciation, it again becomes fit for devotional exercises.

5. When going through spiritual exercises (Sâdhanâ) do not associate with those who never concern themselves with matters spiritual. Such people scoff at those who worship God and meditate upon Him and they ridicule piety and the pious. Keep yourself far aloof from them.

6. If a strange animal enters a herd of cows, it is soon driven off by the combined attack of the whole herd. But if it is a cow that enters, the other cows will make friends with her by mutual licking of bodies. Similarly, when a devotee meets with another devotee, they talk of spiritual matters, rejoice in each other's company and feel loath to separate ; but a devotee does not care to associate with a scoffer.

7. If one wishes to drink water from a shallow pond, one should gently take the water from the surface and not disturb it. If it is disturbed, the sediment will rise up from the

bottom and make the water muddy. Similarly, if you desire to know God, have faith in your *Guru* (spiritual guide) and steadily go on with devotional practices. Do not waste your energies over useless scriptural discussions and disputations. The little brain, you know, easily gets muddled.

8. The evil spirit is exercised by throwing charmed mustard seeds on the patient, but if the spirit has entered into the seeds themselves how can such seeds remove the spirit ? If the mind wherewith you are to contemplate the Deity be attached to worldly things, how can you expect to be successful in your religious devotions ?

9. Let there be harmony between your thought and speech ; that is the right form of spiritual exercise. Otherwise, if you say, "O Lord ! Thou art my all-in-all," while you are throughly convinced that the world is your all-in-all, all your devotional exercises are bound to be fruitless.

10. None can enter the Kingdom of Heaven if there be the least trace of desire

in him, just as a thread can never enter the eye of a needle if there be any slight detached fibre at its end. When the mind ceases to be moved by desires and thus becomes pure, then it is that one can realize the Absolute.

11. The aspirant for the Kingdom of Heaven must on no account be attached to lust or gold. It is impossible that one should ever become perfect (*siddha*) if there be the least attachment of the kind. Of the grains of paddy which are fried in a pan containing sand, those few that leap out of the pan and burst outside do not bear any mark of burn. The rest of the grains, which are in the pan itself, are all charred by the hot sand in some spot or other.

12. Let no one practise devotional exer- cises (*sâdhanâ*) having any ulterior object (*e.g.*, wealth, worldly honours, birth of a son, &c.) in view. He who seeks the Lord alone, has his desire fulfilled.

13. Just as an object cannot be reflected by water if it be agitated by the wind, so God cannot be reflected by the mental lake, if it be

agitated by the wind of desires. The human
mind becomes ruffled by the process of breath-
ing ; hence it is that the Yôgi first concentrates
his mind by regulating his breath before he
begins meditating upon God.

14. He alone enters the Kingdom of
Heaven who is not a thief of his own thoughts.
In other words, guilessness and simple faith
are the roads to that Kingdom.

15. On coming across a snake, it is usual
for one to say, "O Mother Manasâ (the
Goddess of snakes), do hide your face and
show me only your tail." Similarly, on meeting with a young woman you should salute
her, addressing her at the same time as your
mother and instead of looking at her face,
you should look towards her feet. If you do
so, you shall be free from the fear of tempta-
tion or fall.

16. Every Sannyâsin (a person who has
renounced the world) and every lover of
God should regard womankind, whether
chaste or the reverse, as the manifestation of
the Divine Mother.

17. He alone possesses the spirit of true renunciation, who on meeting a young woman in a lonely place turns away from her, saluting her in his mind as his own mother. But he who acts in this way in the public gaze merely for the sake of show, cannot be said to be a genuine *tyâgi* (a person without worldly attachment).

18. The seed of egoism cannot be destroyed easily. When the head of a goat is severed from its body, the trunk moves about for some length of time, till the goat dies hard. Even so does a person's egoism.

19. It is very hard to get rid of one's egoism. The cup in which the juice of the garlic or onion is kept, retains the strong odour of the bulb, though it may be washed hundreds of times. Similarly, some trace of a person's egoism is always left behind.

20. What is the sign of a genuine *sannyâsin* (one who has renounced the world) or *tyâgi* (one who is without worldly attachment) ? Both must be entirely unconnected with lust and gold. Should either feel

an attachment for gold or be troubled by
pollution, even in a dream, all his spiritual
exercises would come to naught.

21. God is like the Divine-Tree (*Kalpataru*), which gives whatever one asks of it.
So one should be careful to give up all worldly
desires when one's mind has been purified by
religious exercises. Just hear a story: A
certain traveller came to a large plain in the
course of his travel. As he had been walking
in the sun for a good many hours, he was thoroughly exhausted and was heavily perspiring;
so he sat down in the shade of a tree to take
a little rest. Presently he began to think
what a comfort it would be, could he but get
a soft bed there to sleep upon. The traveller
had no idea that he was sitting under a Divine-
Tree. As soon as the above thought arose in
his mind, he found a nice bed by his side. He
felt very much astonished, but all the same,
stretched himself on it. Now he thought to himself how pleasant it would be were a young damsel to come there and gently stroke his legs. No
sooner had the thought arisen in his mind than

he found a young damsel sitting near his feet and stroking his legs. The traveller felt supremely happy. Presently he felt very hungry and thought within himself, "I got whatever I have wished for ; could I not then get some food ?" Instantly he found various kinds of delicious food spread before him. He at once fell to eating, and then having helped himself to his heart's content, stretched himself again on his bed. He now began to revolve in his mind the events of the day. While thus occupied he thought to himself : "If a tiger should attack me all of a sudden !" In an instant a large tiger jumped upon him, broke his neck and began to drink his blood. In this way the traveller lost his life. Such is the fate of men in general. If during your meditation you pray for men or money or worldly honours, your desires are no doubt satisfied to some extent, but mind, there is the dread of the tiger hidden behind the gifts you gets Those tigers—disease, bereavement, loss of honour and wealth, &c., are a thousand times more terrible than the living tiger.

22. A certain person had a sudden fit
of renunciation. He told his friends that the
world had ceased to have any attraction for
him and he wished at once to retire into solitude to meditate upon God. They readily
assented to his laudable proposal. So he left
home and having reached a lonely place went
through austere devotional exercises for twelve
long years. Having by this means acquired
some psychic power he returned home. His
friends were very glad to meet him after so long
a time and in course of conversation, asked
him what knowledge he had acquired by his
long penance. He smiled, as advacing towards
an elephant that was passing by, he touched
its body and pronounced these words : "Die
instantly, you elephant." Instantly the animal
ceased to show any sign of life. Shortly afterwards he touched the elephant again and pronounced these words : "Be alive, you elephant,"
and directly the animal was alive once more.
He next went to the bank of the river that
flowed by his house, and having repeated some
mantras (occult formulæ), walked across the

river and returned in the same way. His friends were very much struck by his performances ; all the same they could not forbear from saying to him, "Brother, your penance has been to no purpose. What is it to you whether the elephant lives or dies ? And as for walking on the river, which you have accomplished after twelve years' hard labour, we do it by paying a pice to the boatman. So you see you have simply wasted your labours." These sarcastic comments brought him to his senses and he asked himself, "Really, what good have my psychic powers done me ?" With these words he left home once more—this time to seek for God by austere devotional exercises.

23. It is foolish of think oneself very clever. The crow is very clever in his way and no doubt thinks himself so. All the same he has to live upon ordure. Similarly, the pettifogger only brings ruin upon himself by what he thinks to be wordly wisdom, but which is really nothing better than low cunning.

24. One day standing on the bank of the

Ganges with a rupee in one hand and a lump of clay in the other, I reasoned within myself and came to the conclusion that there was no difference between the two ; so I threw both away into the river. But this made me somewhat anxious, lest I should have given offence to the Mother *Lakshmi* (the Goddess of wealth), who might stop my daily bread ! A second thought presently arose in my mind ; accordingly I said, "O Mother *Lakshmi*, do Thou make my heart Thy throne ; I do not want any of Thy wealth."

25. Two are the occasions when the Lord smiles. First, when He finds two brothers dividing with a rope the land left by their father and saying, "This side is mine, that side is yours." Secondly, when the patient is dangerously ill and the physician says to his weeping friends, "Fear not ; I take it upon.myself to see that the patient gets well." The fool of a physician does not know that no human power can save him whom the Lord chooses to destroy.

26. The Lord *Sri Krishna* had said to

Arjûna, "If you possess even one of the eight psychic powers (*siddhis*), you will never know Me in My highest mood." The genuine devotee must not, therefore, desire any of these powers.

27. A rich Marwari, (an inhabitant of Marwar in Rajputna) Lakshminarayana by name, who loved the company of holy men, once paid a visit to Sri Ramakrishna. They had a long discussion about the *Vedânta* and other scriptural subjects. Lakshminarayana was so very satisfied with Sri Rama-krishna's exposition that before he left his presence, he offered to pay ten thousand rupees for his *sevâ* (service). The proposal acted like a hard blow on his head and he very nearly swooned away. As soon as he recovered himself he addressed Lakshminarayna, after the manner of a little boy, his tone betraying his utter disgust at the proposal made to him, "Get out of this room at once, you fellow! you want to drag me down into the phenomenal world by tempting me with riches!" Lakshmi-narayana, who was an admirer of Sri Rama-krishna, felt a little disconcerted for a moment

and then remarked, "Sir, you are still slightly below the mark." Sri Ramakrishana said, "How so ?" His admirer replied, "A perfect saint makes no distinction between the acceptability and unacceptability of anything offered to him. He is not pleased if anything be given him, nor he is displeased if anything be taken away from him." Sri Ramakrishna gave him a slight smile and then explained to him the position : "Look here," said he, "if there be a spot, however slight, on the mirror, it cannot best reflect your face ; similarly, it is not meet that there should be a trace even of lust or gold in a pure mind." His admirer replied, "Well said ; the amount might be held on your behalf by your nephew Hridaya, who attends on you." Sri Ramakrishna replied, "No, that even might not be done. For suppose, I were to ask Hridaya to pay some-thing to anyone or feel inclined to spend something over any particular object and he should object, the thought might naturally come to me—'the money is not his, he holds it merely on my behalf' ; such egoism, too, is to

5

be deprecated." Lakshminarayana heard this explanation with wonder and went home highly pleased with the unforeseen renunciation of Sri Ramakrishna.

28. It is foolish to brag of riches. If you say you are rich, know that there are richer and richer men than you. At nightfall, when the glow-worms make their appearance, they think that it is they that light up the world ; but their vanity passes away as soon as the stars appear. Then the stars begin to think that it is they that light up the world ; but as soon as the moon is up, they fade away as it were in shame. Now the moon in her turn thinks that it is she that makes the world smile with her beam. But presently on the appearance of the sun she loses her lustre and soon becomes invisible. If those who think themselves rich, ponder over these natural facts, they can never boast of their riches again.

29. "All for a single piece of rag (kaupina)." A sâdhû (holy man) under the instruction of his gûrû (spiritual guide), built

for himself a small shed, thatched with leaves,
at a distance from the haunts of men. He
began his devotional exercises in this hut.
Now, every morning after ablution he would
hang his wet cloth and the rag he wore under
it, on a tree close to the hut, to dry them ;
but on his return from the neighbouring
village, which he would visit to beg for his
daily food, he found that the rats had cut
holes in his rag, so that the next day he was
obliged to go to the village for a fresh one. A
few days later, the *sâdhû* spread his rag on the
roof of his hut to dry it and then went to the
village to beg as usual. On his return he
found that the rats had torn his rag into
shreds. He felt much annoyed and thought
within himself, "Where shall I go again to beg
for a rag ? Whom shall I ask for one ?" All
the same, he saw the villagers the next day
and represented to them the mischief done by
the rats. Having heard all he had to say, the
villagers said, "Who will keep you supplied
with cloth every day ? Just do one thing—
keep a cat ; it will keep away the rats." The

sâdhû forthwith secured a kitten in the village and carried it to his hut. From that day the rats ceased to trouble him and there was no end to his joy. The *sâdhû* now began to tend the useful little creature with great care and feed it on the milk begged from the village. After some days, a villager said to him, "*Sâdhûji*, you require milk every day; you can supply your want for a few days at most by begging; who will supply you with milk all the year round? Just do one thing —keep a cow. You will satisfy your own comforts by drinking her milk and you can give some to your cat." In a few days the *sâdhû* procured a milch-cow and had no occasion to beg for milk any more. By and by the *sâdhû* found it necessary to beg for straw for his cow. He had to visit the neighbouring villages for the purpose, but the villagers said, "There are lots of uncultivated land close to your hut, just cultivate the land and you shall not require to beg for straw for your cow." Guided by their advice, the *sâdhû* took to tilling the land. By and by he had to

engage some labourers and later on found it
necessary to build barns to store the crop in.
He now passed his days just like a busy house-
holder. After some time his *gûrû* came to see
him. Finding himself surrounded by goods
and chattels, the *gûrû* felt puzzled and enquired of a servant, "An ascetic used to live
here in a hut ; can you tell me where he has
removed himself ?" But the servant did not
know what to say in reply. So the *gûrû* ven-
tured to enter into the house where he met
his disciple. The *gûrû* said to him, "My
son ! What is all this ?" The disciple in
great shame fell at the feet of his *gûrû* and
said, "My Lord ! All for a single piece of
rag !" and then described in detail everything
that had happened. All his worldly attachments vanished at the sight of his *gûrû*, whom
he followed directly, leaving his goods and
chattels behind.

CONDITIONS FAVOURABLE FOR DEVOTIONAL EXERCISES

1. At the beginning one should try to concentrate one's mind in a lonely place; otherwise the mind may be distracted by many things. If we keep milk and water together, they are sure to get mixed; but if the milk be churned into butter, the butter instead of getting itself mixed with water will float upon it. So, when by long practice a man has brought his mind under his control he can constantly meditate upon God, whether he be in a lonely place or not.

2. Without single-minded devotion (nișthā), God cannot be realised. As the woman who is fully devoted to her husband is called sati (chaste) and possesses his love, so that the man who is fully devoted to his ideal (Ișta) possesses His grace and realises Him.

3. On being asked, "How old is the

Moon to-day ?" *Hanumân* (the Monkey-God) replied : "I do not know anything about the days of the week, or the phases of the moon, or the position of the stars ; I know only the lotus-feet of Sri Ramachandra."

4. The mind, the forest and the retired corner are three places for meditation.

5. How could you expect to get rid of a serious illness without rest and solitude ? It is the typhoid that the worldly man is suffering from and you keep a large jar of water and savoury pickle in the patient's room ! Lust is like a pickle and the desire to enjoy worldly things is like a jar of water. How could you expect to shake off your illness under the circumstances ? One should retire into solitude for some time and practise devotional exercises. There is nothing to be afraid of if one returns home after one has made a thorough recovery by adopting the above remedy.

6. In the first stage of one's spiritual life one should try to concentrate one's mind by going into solitude to meditate upon Him ;

when by constant practice the mind has been brought under control, one can meditate any-where one chooses. A young plant requires to be protected with care by a fence, or else goats and cows will eat it up ; but when the same plant grows into a large tree with a stout stem, the cows or goats tied to it will not injure it.

7. A certain young disciple asked Sri Ramakrishna, "Lord, how can one conquer lust ?" Sri Ramakrishna smiled and said, "Look upon all women as your own mother ; never look at the face of a woman, but look towards her feet. All evil thoughts will then fly away."

8. The quality of forbearance is of the highest importance to every man. He alone is not destroyed, who possesses this quality. In the Bengali alphabet no other letter occurs in three different forms except *Sha*. The three forms—*Ṣ, Sh* and *S* : all mean the same *viz.,* forbear.

9. There is no quality higher than for-bearance, which all should cultivate. A black-

smith's anvil remains immovable under the countless blows of his heavy hammer, so should everyone with a firm determination endure all that is said or done by others.

10. If a savoury bait be thrown into a pond the fishes hasten to it from all quarters. The faith of a devotee acts in similar manner in respect of God. Attracted by his faith the Lord quickly comes to His devotee and reveals Himself to him.

11. The insect which appears in the rainy season rushes towards a flame and would rather die in the flame than return to darkness. Similarly, the devotee hastens to where holy men live and converse about God. He keeps himself aloof from the worthless attractions of the world and spends his time in devotional exercises.

12. Pârvati once asked Mahâdêva, "O Lord ! what is the clue to the knowledge of God ?" Mahâdêva replied, 'Faith is the only clue to it.' You cannot know God unless you have implicit and firm faith in the teachings of your spiritual guide (gûrû).

13. He is born to no purpose who, having the rare privilege of being born a man, is unable to realise God in this life.

14. The worldly man is like the spring-cushion; so long as you sit on the cushion you keep it squeezed; leave your seat, the cushion will resume its original shape. Similarly, the pious sentiments which a worldly-minded man feels while in the company of the good and the holy, disappear as soon as he leaves such company and his mind becomes as impure as before.

15. Once a person comes to believe in the power of His holy name and feels inclined to constantly repeat it, neither discrimination nor devotional exercises of any sort are necessary for him. All doubts are set at rest, the mind becomes pure, the Lord Himself is realised through the force of His holy name.

16. God is to be reached through child-like faith and guilelessness. A certain person, on coming across a *sâdhû* (holy man), humbly begged him for instruction. The *sâdhû*'s advice was: "Love God with all your heart

and soul." The enquirer replied, "I have never seen God, nor do I know anything about Him ; how is it possible that I should love Him ?" The holy man enquired whom the other loved most. The answer was, "I have no-body to care for. I have a sheep and that is the only creature I love." The *sâdhû* said : "Then tend the creature and love it with all your heart and soul and always remember that the Lord abides in it." Having given this advice the *sâdhû* left the place. The enquirer now began to tend the sheep with loving care, fully believing that the Lord abides in the creature. After a long time the *sâdhû* during his return-journey sought out the person he had advised and enquired how he was getting on. The latter saluted the *sâdhû* and said, "Master, I am all right, thanks to your kind instruction. Much good has come to me by following the line of thought prescribed by you. Time and again I see a beautiful figure with four hands within my sheep and I find supreme bliss in that."

17. The association of pious men is like

water in which rice has been washed. Just as the intoxication caused by wine is dissipated by rice-water, similarly the only way to dissipate the intoxication caused by the wine of desire is the association of the pious.

18. Sri Ramakrishna would compare *sâdhûs* (holy men) to snakes. As the snake never digs a hole for itself, but lives in holes made by a rat, similarly a *sâdhû* builds no house for himself, but lives in other men's houses, if there be need.

19. As one thinks of cases and courts on seeing a lawyer, and of diseases and medicines on seeing a physician, so one remembers his God and the here-after on seeing a pious devotee.

PERSEVERANCE IN DEVOTIONAL
EXERCISES (SÂDHANÂ)

1. If a single dive into the sea do not bring to you the pearl, do not conclude that the sea is without pearls. Countless are the pearls hidden in the sea. So, if you fail to see God directly after you have finished a few devotional exercises, do not lose heart. Go on patiently with your exercises and you are sure to obtain divine grace at the proper time.

2. There is a kind of oyster that constantly floats about on the surface of the sea with its shell wide-open until it succeeds in catching a drop of the marvellous Svâti-rain (Svâti is the star Arcturus). Then it dives down to the sea-bed and does not come up again. Similarly, the true and the earnest aspirant, having got the precious logos (mantram) from his spiritual guide, dives down into the bottomless sea of devotion, without throwing a glance at anything worldly.

3. As to approach to a wealthy man, one has to ingratiate oneself with the guards who keep the gate, so to reach the Almighty one must practise many devotions, keep the company of the pious and have recourse to various other means.

4. A wood-cutter led a very miserable life by selling fire-wood, which he brought from a forest. One day as he was carrying home a load of thin fire-wood, he was accosted by a stranger who advised him *to go a-head*. The next day he followed the advice and went further into the forest and had his reward, for he met with an abundance of large trees in that part of the forest. He cut down as many logs as his strength permitted and by selling them made much larger profit than he had ever made before. The next day he thought to himself, "I have been advised to go a-head ; why not go further a-head to-day ?" He did as he thought and that day reached a part of the forest which was full of sandal-wood trees. He took away with him as many sandal-logs as he could carry and by selling them in the

market made a large profit. The next day he again remembered the stranger's advice and resolved to make a further advance. That day he came upon a copper-mine. But this did not check his further advance ; day after day as he advanced further and further, he got at silver-mines, gold-mines and diamond-mines and at last grew enormously rich. Such is the case also with the path of spirituality. One should constantly go a-head and must not think that one - has achieved every-thing as soon as one has seen a few visions or the Light Divine or acquired some psychic powers.

5. What should a man do if he be in-formed that large fishes abound in a certain pond ? Were he first to visit those who had fished in it and enquire of them if his infor-mation were correct, and if so, what would be the most suitable bait, and were he to spend his time in collecting information of like nature, he would never be fishing. What he should do is to go to the pond, throw his line and wait with patience. Presently he will find the fishes nibbling at the bait and in due course

he will succeed in hooking a large fish. Even so with matters spiritual. One should put implicit trust in what holy men and devotees say, and having thrown the bait of devotion one should wait with the rod and line of patience.

6. A certain person said to Sri Ramakrishna, "Sir, I have gone through a long course of devotional exercises but everything is as dark as before. They are of no use to persons of my kind." Sri Ramakrishna gave him a slight smile and said, "Look here ; the hereditary agriculturist does not leave off tilling the soil though it may not rain for twelve consecutive years ; while those who do not strictly belong to that class but take to agriculture in the hope of making large profits, are discouraged by one season of drought. The true believer does not give up repeating His holy name and proclaiming His glory, if even with his life-long devotion he fails to see God."

7. Long must you struggle in the water before you learn to swim ; similarly, many a struggle must you pass through before you can hope to swim on the ocean of Divine Bliss.

YEARNING FOR GOD

1. How should one love God ? If one's love for Him is as strong as the three following attachments put together, *viz.*, the attachment of a worldly man to things of the world, the attachment of a miser to his hoard and the attachment of a chaste and devoted wife to her husband—one is sure to see God.

2. A mother has several children. To one she has given a toy, to another a doll, to a third some sweets, so that absorbed in these things they all forget their mother. But among them the child who throws away his playthings and cries after the mother, "Where is my Mamma ?"—draws her to himself. She runs quickly to him and takes him up in her arms and soothes him. So, O man ! you are absorbed in thoughts of lust and gold. When you throw them off and cry for the Divine Mother, She will come to you and take you up in Her arms.

6

3. Men weep rivers of tears because a son is not born to them or because they cannot get riches. But who sheds even a drop of tear because he has not been fortunate enough to see the Lord or possess love enough for him ?

4. The Lord Jesus was one day walking along the sea-shore when a devotee approached Him and asked Him, "Lord, how can one attain God ?" The Lord directly descended into the sea with the enquirer, whom He plunged under the water. After a short time He released him and raising him by the arm asked him, "How didst thou feel ?" The devotee replied, "I felt as though my last moment were come—the condition was desperate." Upon this the Lord said, "Thou shalt see the Father when thy yearning for Him will be as intense as thy yearning for a breath of air just now."

5. A child beseeches its mother with importunities for pice, weeping and even beating her ; the man who, like the child, cries bitterly after the Mother Divine, with the firm

conviction that She is his very own, has his reward. The Blessed Mother can no longer remain hidden from him.

6. Speaking about his own yearning for the Divine Mother, Sri Ramakrishna would say : "On hearing the united sound of gongs, bells, cymbals &c, at the evening-worship of the Goddess in the Dakshineswar Temple I would run to the bank of the Ganges and cry out to the Divine Mother, 'O Mother ! another day is gone, but Thou hast not yet vouchsafed to reveal Thyself to Thy son !'"

7. When a man is thirsty, does he refuse to drink of the Ganges-water because it is turbid and does he proceed directly to dig a tank to provide himself with drinking water ? He who has no thirst for religion, goes about attacking all religions and raising endless discussions about them. One who is thirsty has no time for nice discrimination.

LOVE OF GOD AND GOD-CONSCIOUSNESS
(BHAKTI AND BHÁVA)

1. *Heeré-mati* (diamonds and pearls) worth lacs of rupees can be had in the market, but how few are the persons with *Krishné-mati* (devotion to the Lord *Sri Krishna*) !*

2. An ordinary plate of glass will not receive an impression of anything, but a photographic plate (which is overlaid with a coating of chemicals) will. Similarly, in the pure heart, overlaid with a coating of the love of God, is reflected the image of the Almighty. No reflection takes place in the pure heart if there be no love of God as well.

3. "Well, what is *Préma* (intense love of God) ?" It is when on uttering the sweet name of *Hari* (the Lord) one entirely forgets the external world—nay even one's own body, so very dear to one.

---

* There is a pun on the word *mati*, which in Bengali means both 'pearls' and 'inclination'.

4. First, God-consciousness (Bhāva), next, ecstatic love (Prēma) and last of all forgetfulness of self (Bhâva-samâdhi). You know that when a number of people begin chanting the name of the Lord they at first repeat the entire sentence, "Nitāi āmār mātā hāti (My Nitai is a mad elephant) ; presently if God-consciousness (Bhāva) comes on any of the group, he can repeat only the word hāti (elephant) ; later on, as he passes into ecstasy (Prēma), hs is unable to repeat even the whole of that word ; lastly, when the self is entirely forgotten (i. e., in Bhāva-samâdhi) he can utter only the first syllable hā. In this way by degrees he becomes speechless and ceases to have any consciousness of the external world.

5. As an elephant entering into a hut soon makes it totter to its foundation and at last pulls it down, similarly, an intense love for the Lord pulls down the frail house called the human body.

6. The true devotee says, "Lord, I am the yantra (machine), Thou art the yantri

(one who works the machine); I am the room,
Thou art the tenant; I am the chariot, Thou
art the charioteer; I speak just as Thou makest
me speak; I act as Thou makest me act; I
behave as Thou makest me behave."

7. Love of God, by itself, reduces the
amount of one's secular work. One who
loves the Lord cannot at the same time love
secular work. He who has once tasted the
drink prepared with the sugar-candy, does
not care for that made with molasses.

8. Rituals and other ceremonial work
(*Sandhyâ-ânhika*) are necessary only so long
as one does not acquire a true love for God;
that is, so long as tears of ecstasy do not flow
and the hairs of the body do not stand on end
at the mere mention of His name.

9. In *Yâtrâs* (old-fashioned theatrical
perfomances) you have seen that so long as
the clatter of music continues and the players
sing at the top of their voices, "O *Krishna*,
do come; let us have a sight of Thee!"—the
Krishna in the play does not in the least mind
the summons; he goes on with his smoke

and chat, and leisurely puts on his costume.
When all noise ceases and the *Rishi* (seer)
Nārada in a soft and loving tone begins his
song, "I die, O *Govinda*—my life and soul !"
—*Krishna* can no longer help coming forward ;
he hurriedly appears on the stage. Similar
is the case with an aspirant. So long as he
cries aloud : "Lord ! do come ; reveal Thyself to me !"—know that the Lord is far away
from him. When the Lord will actually reveal
Himself to him, he will be quiet and full of
peace. When the aspirant calls on the Lord,
his heart full of love, He can no longer defer
showing Himself to his devotee.

10. *Ahalyā* said to *Sri Rāmachandra* :
"O *Rāma* ! I do not mind being born of a
sow, but let me not be deprived of constant
love and reverence for Thee. I do not require
any other boon of Thee."

MEDITATION (DHYĀNA)

1. Do you know how a man of *Sāttvika* (pure) nature meditates ? He meditates in the night, seated upon his bed, within the curtain. The people of his house think that he is asleep. A pure-hearted devotee never makes any outward show of his devotion.

2. In the course of his meditation an aspirant sometimes falls into a kind of sleep that goes by the name of *Yoga-nidrā*. On such occasions many aspirants see some kind of divine visions.

3. When you sit in meditation, be wholly absorbed in God. During a perfect meditation one would not know if a bird were to perch upon one. When I used to sit in meditation in the theatre-hall (*nātya mandira*) of the temple of the Mother *Kāli*, sparrows and other little birds would perch upon my body and move about in sport. Everybody said so.

DEVOTIONAL PRACTICE (SĀDHANĀ) AND FOOD

1. He who lives upon *havishya-anna* (*i.e.,* rice mixed with clarified butter, &c., considered a pure food) but does not desire to attain God, for him such food is as bad as beef. On the other hand, he who eats beef, but tries to attain God, for him beef is as good as *havishya-anna.*

2. The mother-in-law of the late Bijoy Krishna Goswami, of revered memory, one day came to pay her respects to Sri Rama-krishna, who remarked, "You are following the right path; although you live in the world, your heart is given to the Lord." The lady said : "How so ? I do not see that I am advancing; I cannot yet eat the leavings of others." Sri Ramakrishna said, "What do you say ? Is the ability to eat the leaving of others the goal to be reached ? The dog and the jackal devour such leavings, but do they acquire *Brahma-Jnâna* (knowledge of God Absolute) in consequence ?"

DIVINE GRACE

1. A match lighted in a dark room dis-
perses all at once the accumulated darkness of
centuries. Similarly, a single gracious glance
of the Lord washes away the accumulated sins
of innumerable births.

2. When the *malaya* breeze blows, all
trees having stamina in them are turned into
sandal trees ; but those which have no stamina
(*e.g.*, bamboo, plaintain &c.) remain un-
changed. So when Divine Grace descends, men
having germs of piety and goodness in them
are changed at once into saints ; but worthless
and worldly men are not easily changed.

3. Children go on with their play in the
nursery so long as their mother is not by.
Neither fear nor anxiety troubles them, so
deeply absorbed are they in their play-things.
But as soon as the mother comes in, they
throw away their toys and run towards her
crying, "Mamma ! Mamma !" You too are now

absorbed in playing with the worldly toys of
wealth, honour and fame ; you too feel quite
happy and know no fear or anxiety. But if
you can once get a glimpse of the all-blissful
Mother, you will have no inclination for
wealth, honour or fame ; you will run to Her
throwing all your playthings away.

4. It is the nature of the child to soil itself
with dirt and mud, but its parents do not
allow it to remain dirty. Similarly, how-so-ever
polluted a man may become by living amidst
the attractions of the phenomenal world, the
Lord creates means for his purification.

THE STATE OF A PERFECT MAN
(SIDDHA)

1.   Iron if once converted into gold by the touch of the philosopher's stone (sparsha-mani), may be kept buried in the ground or thrown into a heap of rubbish, it always remains gold. Similar is the state of him who has attained God. Whether he dwells in the midst of worldly attractions or in the solitude of the forests, nothing will contaminate him.

2.   The steel sword is turned into a golden sword by the touch of the philosopher's stone and though it retains its former form, it becomes incapable of injuring anybody. Similarly, although the outward appearance of the man who has touched the lotus-feet of the Lord is not changed, yet he cannot harm anybody.

3.   A certain man asked Sri Ramakrishna, "What is the state which a perfect man (siddha-purusha) attains ?" He replied, "As potato or brinjal becomes soft when boiled

(*siddha*),* so a man becomes tender when he attains perfection. He loses all egoism."

4. Sri Ramakrishna would point towards his own body and say : "This is merely a receptacle, but it serves as the abode of the Mother Divine."

5. The hymns of Ramaprasada never lose their freshness. Do you know why ? It is because the Divine Mother abode in his heart when he composed them.

6. The state of perfection (*siddha-avasthâ*) is attained in this world in many ways, *e.g.*, there are the *Svapna-siddha*, the *Mantra-siddha*, the *Hathât-siddha* and the *Nitya-siddha*.

7. The *Svapna-siddhas* are those who attain perfection by getting *mantram* (the name of the Ideal Deity) in a dream and repeating the *mantram*. The *Mantra-siddhas* are those who get the *mantram* from a properly qualified *gûrû* (spiritual guide) and

---

* There is a pun on the word Siddha, which in Bengali means both perfected and boiled.

perform devotional exercises according to his directions. They become perfect in this way. The *Hathât-siddhas* are those who suddenly attain perfection through the grace of a saint. The *Nitya-siddhas* are those who are perfect even from their birth. They are like the gourd or pumpkin creeper, which bears fruit first and then its flowers.

8. As water flows out freely under a bridge but never stagnates, so money flows out freely through the fingers of 'the Free,' nothing being retained in their hands. Persons of this class do not possess the least worldly wisdom.

9. "To him who is perfect in meditation, salvation is very near," is an old saying. Do you know when a man becomes perfect in meditation ? When, as soon as, he sits down to meditate, he loses himself in the sea of spirituality.

10. How does the emancipated soul live in the world.? He lives in the world like the diver-bird. It dives into water, but the water does not wet its plumage ; the few drops of

water which may possibly stick to its body are
easily jarked off when it once laps its wings.

11. The magnatic needle always points
to the North, whatever the direction of the
ship's sailing ; hence it is that the ship does
not lose her course. If the mind of man be
always turned towards God, he will steer clear
of every danger.

12. The flint may remain for centuries
under water, still it does not lose its property ;
take it out of water and strike it with steel,
a bright spark will be at once produced.
Similarly, the true devotee never loses his
faith and love, although he may live amidst
all the impurities of the world. He becomes
intoxicated with the love of God as soon as
he hears His name.

13. One becomes as one thinks. They
say that by constantly thinking of a particular
kind of insect (bhramara-keeta), a cockroach
is itself transformed into that insect. Similarly,
he who constantly thinks of the Bliss Absolute
becomes himself full of Bliss.

14. A drunkard under the influence of

drink now wraps his only piece of cloth round his head, now taking the cloth under his arm, walks about naked like a child. The ways of a saint do not differ outwardly from those of a drunkard.

15. Egoism is like the petal of the lotus or the leaf of the cocoa-palm or of the arecapalm. When the petals of the lotus or the palm-leaves drop off, a scar or mark is left behind. Similarly, although egoism may have left a person, it is sure to leave a mark behind. But such egoism cannot injure anybody ; it merely enables one to continue to live in the world by ministering to one's physical wants—eating, sleeping &c.

16. Just as a ripe mango falls of itself, similarly, when the perfection of knowledge is reached by a man, all fetters fall-off of themselves. It is wrong for a man to forcibly throw off caste-distinctions.

17. There are three kinds of quality (gûna): Sattva (purity), Rajas (the quality which leads to work with attachment) and Tamas (ignorance). But not one of these can reach the Lord. Just hear a story

illustrating the point : A man was going
through a forest when he was attacked by
three robbers, who despoiled him of everything he had. One of the robbers then said,
"What is the good of sparing this fellow ?"
and forthwith lifted his axe to behead him.
Another robber opposed the first and said,
"I say, do not kill the fellow ; what is the
good of killing him ? Better leave him here
with his arms and legs tied up." This was
agreed to and all the three fell upon their
victim, bound him hand and foot and then
left the place. After some time one of the
robbers returned to the prisoner and said,
"Alas ! how hurt you must be ; I shall
instantly release you." Having released him,
the robber desired him to accompany him and
offered to conduct him out of the forest.
When they neared the public road, the robber
told his companion that he would reach home
by taking that road. The grateful fellow
said, "You have saved my life, kindly come
to my house." The robber answered, "No,
I cannot go there—people will know ; I can

7

only point out to you the road to your house ;
that being done, I must depart."

18. How do the emancipated (*mukta-
purusha*) live in the world ? Having no
egoism or will of their own they may be
compared to dry leaves blown about here
and there by the strong wind. The leaves
are sometimes carried to a heap of rubbish,
sometimes to a decent place. Similar is the
case with the emancipated.

19. Sri Ramakrishna used to say : "The
three words which prick me to the core are—
(1) *Guru* (spiritual guide), (2) *Karta* (free
agent) and (3) *Baba* (father). I am not the
free agent ; it is the Lord ; I am merely an
humble instrument in His hands."

20. It is the unboiled paddy grain that
brings forth the shoot : the boiled grain does
not. Similarly, one who has become *siddha*
(boiled, perfect), has not to be born again
in this world.

21. What is that stage which, being
reached, one may be styled a *Paramahamsa*
(the highest soul ; *hamsa* means both *soul*

and *swan*) ? Just as the swan separates the milk from the water with which it has been mixed and drinks only the milk, leaving the water untouched, similarly the *Paramahamsa* accepts only what is Real (*i. e.*, the Absolute) rejecting what is unreal (*i.e.*, the phenomenal world).

22. First ignorance, then knowledge— but both of these are relative. When one comes to know the Absolute, one goes beyond the pale of both ignorance and knowledge. Take a parallel case. When a sharp thorn finds its way into the sole of your foot, you want a second thorn to take out the first; when the first is taken out, you throw away both.

23. After one has reached perfection (*siddhi*) *i.e.*, has seen the Lord, one becomes incapable of doing anything wrong. A perfect dancer never makes a wrong step.

24. When the mind of *Kacha*, son of *Vrihaspati* (the priest of the gods), was returning to the sense-plane after *samâdhi* (perfect meditation), the *Rishis* (seers of old) asked him, "How do you feel now ? *Kacha*

answered, "I feel that God is immanent in everything ; I do not see anything else except Him."

THE HARMONY AMONGST THE
RELIGIONS OF THE WORLD

1. The light of the gas-lamp illumines
the different parts of the town with varying
intensity, but all the lamps receive their
supply of gas from one common source ;
similarly, the religious teachers of all countries
and races receive their inspiration from the
Almighty source.

2. As one can ascend to the roof of a
house by means of a ladder, or a bamboo,
or a staircase, or in various other ways, so
diverse are the ways and means to approach
God. Every religion in the world is one of
the ways to reach Him.

3. There is but one God, but endless
are His names and endless the aspects in
which He may be regarded. Call Him by
any name and worship Him in any aspect
that pleases you, you are sure to see Him.

4. Whoever performs devotional exercises,

with the belief that there is but one *sachchidâ-nanda* (God), is bound to attain Him, no matter in what aspect, name or manner He is worshipped.

5. Different creeds are but different paths to reach the Almighty. Diverse are the means by which this *Kâli* temple may be reached—some come here in boats, some in carriages, some on foot. Similarly, different people attain God by following different creeds.

6. A mother loves all her children equally, but she so arranges the food for them that every-one gets what agrees with him. Similarly, the Lord has provided different forms of worship to suit different men with different capacities and in different stages of spiritual development.

7. The late Keshab Chandra Sen, of revered memory, asked Sri Ramakrishna, "Why is there so much antagonism among the various religious sects, although there is but one God ?" Sri Ramakrishna replied, "Every one says, 'this is my land,' 'this is my house,' and accordingly partitions off what he considers

to be his own property, but no one can parti-
tion off the endless sky overhead. Similarly, a
common man, through ignorance, considers
his own religion to be the best and makes
much useless clamour ; but when his mind
is illumined by true knowledge, all sectarian
quarrel disappears."

8. Q. There being so many sects and
creeds among the Hindus, which sect or creed
should one adopt ?

A. *Pârvati* once asked *Mahâdeva*: "O Lord !
what is the clue to the Bliss Absolute ?" The
Lord replied, "It is Faith ; the peculiarities
of creeds and sects matter nothing." Let
everyone perform with faith the devotional
exercises of his own creed.

9. It is the narrow-minded that abuse
religions other than their own, declare their
own religion to be the best and form sects
(*dal*).* Those whose hearts yearn for the
Lord are above sectarian prejudice and
quarrel ; they spend their time in devotional
exercises. *Dal* (sedge)* does not grow in the

* Dal in Bengali means both 'sect' and 'sedge'.

current of a river, but in tanks and in the stagnant water of small pools.

10. As one large fish is dressed into several dishes (such as, soup, curry, cutlet &c.,) to suit the tastes of the different members of the household, so the Lord, though One, is worshipped by his devotees in different ways according to their individual likings.

11. The Being is the same, only the names are different. For instance, one and the same substance water is called by different names by different people in different countries in different ages. In Bengali the substance is called *jal*, in Hindi *pani*, in English *water* or *aqua*. It is only owing to the ignorance of one another's language that people do not understand one another; otherwise there could not be any misunderstanding.

12. You will advance yourself in whatever way you may meditate upon Him or recite His holy names. The cake made with sugar-candy will taste equally sweet whether it be held straight or oblique, when you eat it.

FRUITS OF ONE'S ACTION

1. Sin, like quicksilver, can never be concealed. If one uses a preparation of mercury even with the greatest secrecy, eruptions are sure to come out some day or other. Similarly, if one commits a sin, one will as surely have to bear the consequence sometime or other.

2. The caterpillar shuts itself up in its own saliva; so the worldly soul gets itself entangled in the meshes of its own actions. But when the caterpillar developes into a butterfly, it rends the cocoon and enjoys freedom; so the worldly soul sets itself free by developing the wings of *viveka* (discrimination) and *vairagya* (non-attachment).

THE RELIGION SUITED TO THE
PRESENT AGE

1. Sri Ramakrishna would often say, "Chant forth the name of *Hari* (God) morning and evening keeping time all the while by clapping your hands ; all your sins and afflictions will then leave you. If you clap your hands standing under a tree, the birds sitting on it will fly away ; so if you chant forth the name of *Hari* clapping your hands at the same time, the birds of evil thoughts will fly away from the tree of your body.

2. In the previous *yûgas* (ages) people used to be attacked with simple fever which a few doses of a decoction of medicinal herbs would cure ; now-a-days fevers are of malarious origin and powerful drugs like Dr. D. Gupta's patent fever-mixture are required to cure them. In past ages people would keep themselves busy with devotional exercises and the rites enjoined by the scriptures ; in this *Kali yûga* (iron age), life resides, so to say, in

food and the mind is weak. The one means
of severing the bonds of attachment to the
world, suited to this age, is the constant repetition of His holy names with the mind fixed
on Him.

3. In whatever way one may fall into the
trough of nectar, one becomes immortal. If one
falls into the trough after many devotional
prayers one becomes immortal ; likewise is he
who is pushed into the trough, Consciously or
unconsciously or even mistakenly, in whatever
way you utter the name of the Lord, you will
acquire the merit of such utterance.

4. For this iron age (*Kali yûga*) it is
communion with God by love, devotion and
self-surrender, as practised by the *Rishi* (Seer)
Nârada, that is most suitable. For the other
yûgas, many hard penances and devotional
practices had been prescribed ; it is very
difficult to perform them with success in this
yûga—the terms of human life is so short
now, not to speak of the malarial fever which
undermines the constitution. How could one
go through hard devotional exercises ?

PREACHING OF RELIGION

1. How is it that a holy prophet is not honoured by his kinsmen at home, but is honoured abroad ? The kinsmen of a juggler who live with him do not crowd round him to see his performances, while strangers living at a distance stand a-gape at his wonderful tricks.

2. The seeds of the thistle-down do not fall to the bottom of the tree ; they are carried by the wind far off and take root there. So the spirit of a great religious teacher manifests itself at a distance and is appreciated there.

3. There is always a shadow under the lamp, while its light illumines the distant objects. So the men in the immediate proximity of a holy prophet do not understand him. Those who live far off are charmed by his spirit.

4. To kill another swords and shields are needed, whilst to kill oneself even a pin

will do ; so to teach others one must study
many sacred books and use many an argument, whilst for self-illumination firm faith in
a single formula will suffice.

5. In that part of the country where I
was born you may often find people measuring
grain lying in a heap. One man goes on
measuring, another stands behind and pushes
the grains on to the first, as soon as he has
nearly finished measuring the portion of the
heap that is within his reach. Much in the
same way the true devotee never lacks his
supply of Truth ; he receives a constant
supply of new ideas from within ; that supply
is never used up.

6. As many warm themselves in the fire
kindled by someone else who has taken the
trouble of collecting the firewood and other
necessary things, similarly, many fix their mind
on the Lord by associating with and following
the instruction of holy men who have come
to know the Lord after many a hard penance.

7. What is true preaching like ? Instead
of preaching to others, if one worship God.

that is enough preaching. He who strives to make himself free is the real preacher. Hundreds come from all sides no one knows whence, to him who is free and receive instruction from him. When a bud opens, bees come from all sides uninvited.

MISCELLANEOUS

1. A certain well-known rich man of Calcutta visited Sri Ramakrishna and in course of conversation with him had recourse to many a tortuous argument. Sri Ramakrishna said : "What is the good of useless discussion ? Go on calling on Him with a simple and believing heart and that will do you good." This advice was not taken in good part by the arrogant visitor who made the rude remark, "Have you yourself been able to know everything ?" Sri Ramakrishna with folded hands and great humility replied, "True, I have not been able to know anything; but then a broomstick, though unclean itself, will cleanse the place it sweeps."

2. *Sri Râmachandra* in course of His travels through the forest, descended into the tank called *Pampâ* for a drink, leaving His bow and arrow stuck into the ground. Coming up He found that a frog was lying covered all over with blood, having been run through by

his bow. He was very sorry and said to the frog, "Why didst thou not make some kind of sound? Then I should have known that thou wast here and thou wouldst not have come to this plight." The frog replied, "O *Ráma*, when I fall into a danger, I call on Thee, saying 'O *Ríma*, save me'; now that Thou Thyself art killing me, whom shall I call on?"

3. A certain devout lady, who was also a devoted wife, lived in the household serving her husband and children with a loving heart and at the same time keeping her mind fixed on the Lord. At her husband's death, as soon as the cremation was over, she broke her glass bangles and wore a pair of gold bracelets in their place. People wondered at her unnatural conduct, but she explained to them, "Hitherto my husband's body had been fragile like the glass bangles. That ephemeral body is gone; he is now like one unchangeable and full in every respect; his body is no longer fragile. So I have discarded the fragile glass bangles and worn ornaments of a permanent nature."

4. The Ganges-water is not to be regarded as water ; nor the dust of *Sri Brindâvana* as dust ; nor the *Mahâprasâda** of *Sri Sri Jagannâtha Deva* as rice. These three are objective manifestations of the Supreme Being.

---

* Rice-offering made to the Lord in the temple at Puri.